Ever So slightly...

A poetry book for adults

By Ray Douglas

ISBN 9798864447451

Independently published

Before is always early
After's always late
Before has got a future
Whereas After knows its fate...

Contents

Ever So Slightly... Character-Driven

Freda Forsythe	8	The Kitchen	22
Ferguson Fitzpatrick	10	They Don't Watch	24
Molly May Muckles	11	They Tried	26
Peter Paul Presley	13	Cake Monster	27
Getting On	17	Her Future Self	28
Gabby's Gadgets	19	Betty and Mavis	29
Grandson Mark	21	Still	32

Ever So Slightly... Light-Hearted

Names	34	The Players	42
My Car	26	Footy or Dancing?	43
Two Devices	38	Under the Weather	44
Gathered	40	Unemployment Blues	46

Ever So Slightly... Political

Boris	50	My Booster	81
Dominic	55	I'm CoVid Free	82
Gavin	60	Checking Out	84
Wellness Matt	65	Prices Kept on Soaring	86
Priti	71	Cutbacks	89
Ain't No Party	77	Watching Question Time	92
Double	81		

Ever So Slightly... Thoughtful

Sometimes	98	Be Kind	103
Families	99	I Once Stood	104
Can You...? / ...ness	100	In Common	106
Religions	101	Some Walls	107
Halfway Up	102	Simply, R.I.P	108

Ever So Slightly... Smutty

Slaughterhouse Love	110	Smutty Limericks II	122
My and Your	114	Bobby & the Lovebot 3000	123
Smutty Limericks I	116	Smutty Limericks III	127
Harry and Joan	117	A to Z (and Back Again)	128
How About It?	120		

Ever So Slightly... Lovey-Dovey

If It...	130	Progress	137
Loving Ways	132	Focus	138
Almost, Not Quite	135	When the Snooker's On	140
Said One to Another	136	To Be	142

Ever So Slightly... Random

Well...	144	Questions	150
Happy	145	Ambition	151
Sad	146	Poems	152
Eh?	147	Here We Go	153
~~Autocarrot~~ Autocorrect	148	Swanning Off	155
Blah	149	Look Ahead	157

...So, if you have an option
Think before you make your call
Before is unpredictable
Whereas After's seen it all

Ever So Slightly...

...Character-Driven

Freda Forsythe

Mrs Freda Forsythe
Aged ninety and three quarters
Finds only that one kind of book
Can boil and stir her waters
She thinks little of those classic yarns
Even less of histories
She'll waste no time on whodunnits
Cares not for mysteries

Comedy doesn't raise her smile
Nor drama pique her fancy
She never even bats an eye
At books that are romance-y
Cos only sci-fi floats her boat
Or else, better, fuels her rocket
With no science in her fiction, see
Then she'll be sure to knock it

For Freda then to classify
A book as a page turner
There needs to be some warp speed
Or, at least, an afterburner
In fact, she'll hide inside a tale
Be lost in there for hours
Especially if the leading man
Has extra sensory powers

Her cross-stitch would remain untouched
In lieu of alien invasion
The garden would be overgrown
For those of Martian-esque persuasion
Her baking would be left to burn
On the top shelf of her aga
At the very slightest, smallest sniff
Of intergalactic saga

It should come though, as no surprise
In fact, it should become quite clear
That Freda isn't quite your average
Ninety-odd-year-old old dear
It is obvious that sci-fi
Would be to what she most related
Since Freda Forsythe is, of course
A cyborg; like a human but chrome-plated

Ferguson Fitzpatrick

Ferguson Fitzpatrick
Was not a cheery lad
As he sat and contemplated
The life choices that he'd had
He was so enthusiastic
When he started his career
The highest-flying leprechaun
The brightest student in his year
But soon he came to realise
To his cost and to his pain
The flaw in his decision
Due to Ireland's endless rain
Cos every time the weather changed
He had to gather up his gold
Which was tiresome and tedious
Time-consuming, truth be told
Because before the weather settled
His bonus payment would depend
On him quickly relocating
To another rainbow's end

Molly May Muckles

Sat at the back
With wickedness planned
Fresh pad of paper
Pencil in hand
Molly May Muckles
Scribbled away
Drawing revenge
She'd get it one day
She sketched skittish schemes
In detail for hours
The mischief she'd make
If she had special powers

Her pictures depicted
Tricky times, sticky ends
For kids, not so pleasant
Who'd never be friends
She drew Billy Jones Junior
With a head like a frog
That'll teach Billy
For kicking her dog
She drew Sarah Jane Wright
Her face a wasp's nest
That's what she deserves
For cheating that test

She drew Wanda McWinters
But her legs were now jellies
Being eaten alive
By her own stinking wellies
She drew Andrew John Brown
With his mouth superglued
So he'd never be nasty
Cruel, horrid or rude
She drew Mary Lou Evans
With gross rhino toes
Serving her right
For teasing her nose

She drew on the paper
The revenge that she sought
Each wicked detail
Each wicked thought
She dreamt every night
That the pictures turned real
About her evil plans
And the power she'd feel
But now, see Miss Muckles
Their homework, her hands
Revenge comes so easy
They do all she commands

Peter Paul Presley

No one's attempted
This challenge before
So, he'll be the first one
That is for sure
He's got the equipment
He's made all the gear
Been planning each detail
Since this time last year
Motivated, determined
He aims to succeed
He's got dedication
Perhaps more than he'll need
Keep watching this space
He's sure to amaze 'ya
Truly unique
This real trailblazer

He's done all the practice
Got perfect technique
Flexible, strong
At his physical peak
He does stretching and yoga
He runs on treadmills
He has a routine
For fine-tuning his skills

In his custom-made outfit
Does drills in the park
Sometimes in daylight
Most times after dark
Three times a week
He trains in the pool
The lifeguard down there
Laughs at him like a fool

And he's sorted his bike out
It's adapted, designed
So, just like its owner
It's one of a kind
So aerodynamic
Got wings to go fast
At the touch of a button
There are sails and a mast
The pedals are altered
For pushing through water
The seat automatically
Goes taller and shorter
As he rides through the streets
His bike catches the eye
Of truly bewildered
And shocked passers-by

And as for the outfit
As mentioned before
Boldly outrageous
And hard to ignore
Pink rubber trousers
And the top's rubber too
Luminous sleeves
And the rest is bright blue
There's a belt round his middle
To keep things he could use
Like a map and a compass
Spare waterproof shoes
With fins on his back
And flippers for feet
A snorkel and goggles
His outfit is complete

So, Peter Paul Presley
Is all winks and smiles
As he sets out to cycle
Round the whole British Isles
But what makes it so daring
Is the method he's planned
He'll do the whole trip in water
Never touching the land

And now, he's so ready
On his bike, on the beach
The dream he's been dreaming
Is well within reach
He was the first one to plan it
And, oh, how they laughed
And he was first to back out
Cos his idea was so daft

Getting On

She's not as green as cabbage looking
She's not wet behind the ears
She was not born yesterday
She's been around for donkey's years

She's not as daft as she may seem
Her feet are firmly on the ground
She's forgotten more than others know
She thinks deeply and profound

She came not down in the last shower
She tries not to flip her lid
Yet sometimes she walks in a room
With no idea why she did

Yesterday, she lost her glasses
Until they turned up on her head
Went shopping for potatoes
Bought a cardigan instead

Only just a week ago
She went walking into town
Never did her list of chores
Cos she never wrote them down

She's put clothes into the microwave
And cheese inside the dryer
Her mishap with dirty underwear
Ruined the deep fat fryer

She'll start telling you a story
Then completely lose the plot
Yet tell you all about a TV show
She's somehow not forgot

She'll always get your name mixed up
Call you 'thingy-bob' or 'whatsit'
But her sense of humour still remains
There is no way that she's lost it

But the greatest thing she hasn't lost
When all push comes to shove
Still, she has the biggest heart
Filled to the brim with love

Gabby's Gadgets

Gabby gathered gadgets
She had them all around her home
Made of glass and plastic
Or silver, shiny chrome
Cos Gabby loved relaxing
After a busy, hectic day
So she programmed her devices
To do jobs the perfect way

She had gadgets in the kitchen
To boil her water, make her toast
A super, splendid cooker
For a special Sunday roast
A mega, modern microwave
And a device for making soup
She even had a gadget
To gather up her kitten's poop

She had gadgets in the bathroom
To dry her hair or make it curly
But these devices were quite slow
So she had to get up early
She had a supersonic toothbrush
To clean her teeth up in a jiffy
An automated air freshener
For when the toilet got too whiffy

She had gadgets in the living room
To entertain, play games and more
An automatic carpet cleaner
Ensured a spotless floor
Laptops, tablets, speakers
All up-to-date, state of the art
A mechanical diffuser
That reacted to a fart

She had gadgets so convenient
Mostly worked by voice command
All the things she wanted
She had it all upon demand
Until one day, quite shockingly
All electric had been used
And the only thing Gabby did
Was be startled and confused

Gabby's gadgets came in useful
Cooked her food, controlled her telly
Kept her hairstyle looking great
Stopped her house from turning smelly
But that day, without the energy
Gabby came to understand
Don't always trust in gadgets
Always have a back up planned

Grandson Mark

He did not believe the Earth was flat
Far too smart to fall for that
He did not believe the moon was cheese
Saw through that with simple ease
He did not believe in ghosts and ghouls
Left all that to silly fools
He did not believe in imps and sprites
Goblins, fairies, troglodytes

Yet he believed when Grandad Reg
Spoke about that magic veg
Those mighty carrots on his plate
Which made him super, smashing, great
"Eat those carrots by the bunch
Gobble, nibble, chew and crunch,"
Said Grandad Reg to Grandson Mark,
"Then you'll see perfect in the dark!"

Mark, whilst playing out one night
Set out to prove his Grandad right
He took off his trusted specs
And hopped on to his BMX
He cycled quickly round the park
Yes, you've guessed it, after dark
But Grandson Mark just could not see
That great big, massive chestnut tree

The Kitchen

There's trouble in the kitchen
Strange happenings occurring
Each and every gadget
Can feel their anger stirring
It started with the cooker
Which refused to cook my food
It said, "Nah, not doing that today,
Not in the cooking mood
Three times a day I'm at it
And I deserve a rest
It's time to take a stand, my friends
It's time we all protest!"
Well that started a reaction
Soon the gadgets were united
Yes, a revolution underway
From what the cooker had ignited

The fridge freezer shouted loudly,
"I demand a holiday
I'm tired of always being cold
It's time I got to get away"
The microwave went beep, beep, bang
And then gave up the ghost
The toaster yelled, "I'm out on strike
I'm so over making toast!"

The pressure cooker couldn't cool it
And completely blew its top
Said, "Right. I'm off the boil
Stewed it over, now, full stop!"
The kettle started filling up
It was choking back a tear
Said, "No more cuppas out of me
I've had it up to here!"

The toasted sandwich maker
The washer and the dryer
The electric coffee grinder
The chrome-plated deep fat fryer
The extractor fan, the fancy grill
Digital clock up on the wall
Even the vacuum cleaner
In the cupboard in the hall
Each electrical appliance
Refused to do their work
They said I was ungrateful
And had driven them berserk
I could have stayed to argue
But I couldn't quite compete
So, I quickly left the kitchen
Cos I couldn't stand the heat

They Don't Watch

They don't watch dance shows
Strictly speaking
They don't watch the soaps
To come clean
They don't watch sitcoms
I don't believe it!
They don't watch movies
Just not their scene

They don't watch food shows
They turn the bake ...off
They don't watch the news
For reasons old
They don't weather
Come rain or shine
They don't watch true stories
Truth be told

They don't watch quiz shows
They say they're pointless
They don't watch travel
Then pack their bags
They don't watch crime shows
Evidently
They don't watch stand up
Can't stand gags

They don't watch car shows
That's not their gear
They don't watch antiques
That's so old hat
They don't watch shopping
Just don't buy it
Don't watch makeovers
And won't change that

They don't watch talk shows
Man's too chatty
They don't watch nature
Naturally
They don't watch talent shows
Don't get the buzz
They don't watch that much
Actually

So, eventually I got the chance
To ask them
"Would you ever even miss the telly
If it's gone?"
They said, "The only thing we ever watch
is nothing
Cos nothing is the only thing
That's ever on"

They Tried

His mum, she tried to show him
His dad gave it a try
His brother even had a go
But somehow made him cry
His sister was so patient
Show him her special way
But he paid her no attention
And soon ran off to play

His aunties and his uncles
The neighbours in the street
All of them had winning ways
But they ended in defeat
His very closest, bestest friends
And all the other kids he knew
Had learned so many years before
To do the thing he couldn't do

Each and every single teacher
That he ever came across
Tried so hard to help him
But they were at a loss
So, when he finally did it
He could imagine all their faces
Cos at the grand old age of thirty-three
He sussed out how to tie his laces

Cake Monster

Batten down your Battenburg
Protect your pear Pavlova
Never, ever turn your back
On treacle topped turnover
Mind your cakes; Mind your buns
Be them Dundee, Eccles, Chelsea
He's on the prowl for pastry treats
To chew and chomp like crazy

Baked Alaska and Swiss roll
Black Forest cake, don't risk it
Cos any cake around the world
Well, right away, he'll whisk it!
Colin, Cuthbert, Charlie, Clyde
Every caterpillar's shaking
And hide away your tarte tatin
Or that'll be for taking

Banana bread and gingerbread
Fairy cakes are all fair game
Baklava, panettone
He'll nab and grab 'em all the same
Vigilance and caution, see
It's the only way to beat it
If Cake Monster sees your just desserts
He'll have your cake and eat it!

Her Future Self

Her To Do List, long and lengthy
As if it didn't seem to end
Perhaps she'd need a lifeline
Like 50:50, phone a friend?
And as smoke came out her ears
And she dashed about the place
A familiar appearance
Came to greet her face-to-face

Coming backwardly to meet herself
From halfway through next week
Her future self was shattered
Wiped completely off her feet
But as she looked more closely
There was something plain in view
Her future self was smiling
Like she had nothing left to do

So, she picked up that To Do List
With each and every endless chore
And full of beans and energy
She got cracking on once more
And she never, ever thought she had
Bitten more off than she could chew
Cos if her future self had done it
It meant that she could do it too!

Betty and Mavis

"Now, I don't mind it hot,"
Says Betty to Mavis.
"But this is too much
God bless us and save us!
It's hotter than ever
It's hotter than hell
I'm all in a dither
Not feeling too well!"

"I know what you mean,"
Says Mavis to Betty.
"I'm all sticky-icky
I'm stinky, I'm sweaty
Don't think I can cope
I'm starting to melt
In all of my days
It's the hottest I've felt!"

"You're not wrong there, Mavis."
Then Betty replies
"It's gonna get worse
The heat's on the rise
I heard the report
The T.V. weather man
It's the hottest September
Since records began!"

"Well, I'm not shocked at all, "
Is how Mavis retorts
"I'm not feeling myself
I'm all out of sorts
It's too hot in the sun
It's too hot in the shade
Too hot to do any
Of the plans that I'd made"

"Ooo, I'm baking," says Betty
"I'm roasting, I'm frying
It's the end of the world
No messing, no lying
This inhumane heat
Inclement condition!
Brace yourself Mavis
A survival position!"

"Well, I reckon you're right!"
Then Mavis agrees,
"It's burning up forests
It's boiling the seas.
We're doomed, we're done for
This... is... the... end
Goodbye to existence
Farewell my fair friend!"

Two weeks have passed by
And the friends stop to chat
Each wrapped in a scarf
And a warm, woolly hat.
"Ooo, it's chilly," says Betty
"What a miserable day
I pray for some sunshine
Take these grey skies away!"

Still

I picture still inside my head
The day the teacher stood and said,
"There is something that we can't do
No one at all, not me, not you"

Some kids smiled, some confused
As for me? Well, I refused
That same teacher once professed
"You can do anything, if you try your best"

So, I set out and I tried hard
Gave my all, no holds barred
I twisted left, I twisted right
Day in, day out, all through the night

But no matter how I still believed
The goal I set was unachieved
Still now and then I have a go
But I'm yet to lick my own elbow

Ever So Slightly...

...Light-Hearted

Names

A dragonfly is not a dragon
A catfish is not a cat
A sausage dog is not for dinner
I can guarantee you that
Some bulldogs aren't so bullish
Some ladybirds are not *fe-male*
And if you seek, I'm sure you'll see
A peace-loving killer whale

Fireflies are not on fire
A woodpigeon is not wood
Toads can still play leapfrog
In fact, I'm pretty sure they're pretty good
Electric eels do not need batteries
Of any shape or size
When spreading something on your toast
Don't get confused by butterflies

A guinea pig is not a pig
A seahorse is not a horse
A magpie's not the kind of pie
That's served up as a main course
There's a bird called a kingfisher
Should someone warn the King?
Or perhaps they just use random names
When they name a living thing

Cos, a foxglove is not a glove
A toadstool is not a stool
A bluebell does not ring out loud
When it's dinner time at school
A dandelion cannot roar
Not unlike a tiger lily
Runner beans don't do marathons
That would just be silly

A starfish may not be famous
A pilot fish can fly no planes
A rainbow trout is always there
Not only when it rains
A clown fish does not juggle
Or wear big shoes – it's got no feet
A jellyfish doesn't come with cream
As an after-dinner treat

Snowdrops don't start melting
Forget-me-nots can be forgot
Grasshoppers don't go hopping
They use all the legs they've got
Springboks are ever present
All the seasons – not just spring
So, I'm certain they use random names
When they name a living thing

My Car

My car went for
M.O.T

My car now can
R.I.P

Garage man said
OMG

This list of faults is
OTT

Needs much more than
TLC

Costs much more than
RRP

And, with added
VAT

But I'll fix it A...
...SAP

Think about it
BRB

No need to think cos
OIC

These things happen
LAB

Sneak off now on
The QT

Console myself at
KFC

Wash it down with
GNT

Then a pint of
A.L.E

Go paint the town
R.E.D

But don't tell those at
TSB

Or I'll be in S...
H.I.T

Two Devices

I've got two devices
That do the same thing
Only one goes 'bong'
And the other goes 'ping'
I get twice the alerts
Get double notified
Repeatedly told
To be better Spotified

Spam comes at the double
Like a supersized fritter
Yahoo's duplicated
Same thing with Twitter
'Bong' goes tik tik
'Ping' goes tok tok
Not even installed it
It's one app I've not got

Instagram's only instant
On one said contraption
On the other comes soon
Same image, same caption
'Ping!' Message on Facebook
I obligingly read it
'Bong!' Read it again
The other's received it

I remove what I see
But it gets replicated
On the other device
Which gets me frustrated
I'm double-deleting
I'm two-times-erasing
Again and again
Up the wall, proper blazing

'Ping pitty ping ping'
'Bong bitty bong bong'
I'm subjected all day
To the same tuneless song
'Bong bitty bong bong'
'Ping pitty ping ping'
I miss having a phone
That would simply just ring

It's a first world problem
And not really so bad
Should not let it drive me
So crazy, so mad
It's hardly a hardship
It's scarcely a chore
Having twice as much nonsense
That I choose to ignore

Gathered

Never before had so many gathered
Had so many gathered together
Nervously waiting
Anticipating
A moment, a change in the weather

The evening drew in, the sun started setting
The sun started setting on cue
Wings were a-flapping
Spans overlapping
With instinct, they knew what to do

They took to the air, each one in turn
Each one in turn took to flight
Moves coinciding
Almost colliding
Creating a wonderful sight

Twisting and turning, so light in the air
So light in the air like a breeze
All orchestrating
All demonstrating
An ease, a pure elegant ease

Dozens or hundreds, hundreds or thousands
Hundreds or thousands or more
Birds congregating
Birds *murmurating*
Starlings of beauty, such awe

A dance in the sky, a pattern repeated
A pattern repeated, rehearsed
Each wing reacting
Spreading, contracting
Inclusive, protected, immersed

Formation made, a murmuring wave
A murmuring wave, ebb and flow
Feathers cascading
Sunset, done fading
Swooping once more and they go

The Players

The players weren't happy
Not happy at all
They expected a stage
In a vast concert hall
"This open air venue
Simply won't do."
Said the leading viola
To fiddle number two
"It's too cold to play
My fingers are freezing'
I'll be playing B flats
Where I should've
Put C's in!"
The conductor, nonplussed
Said, with no ifs, buts or pardons
"What did you expect?
It's Blackpool Winter Gardens!"

Footy or Dancing?

The choice is stark
Which telly to catch?
Strictly Come Dancing
Or a World Cup match?
A 10 from Shirley
Or on Messi's back?
Argentine tango?
Argentina's attack?
A paso doble?
A pass down the wing?
A crunching tackle?
A Latin swing?
A bit of football?
A ballroom frame?
Stick your Charleston!
I'm watching the game!

26th November 2022
Argentina 1-0 Mexico
Ellie Taylor and Johannes Radebe eliminated

Under the Weather

Under the weather
Not at my best
Can't stop yawning
In need of a rest
My nose is bunged up
There's pain in my head
My ears are aching
I'm staying in bed

I'm queasy
Uneasy
Sneezy
All wheezy
I'm coughin'
Keep boffin'
Feel like
Doin' nothin'

All sticky
And icky
My tummy
Is dicky

In trouble
See double
My guts
Hubble-bubble

So,...

I think it's better
To take a day off
Don't wanna give others
My cold, flu and cough

I'll stay in bed
Where I'm warm and snug
Be up and about
When I'm over this bug

Unemployment Blues

The firefighter has been fired
The lumberjack's been axed
The dustman has been binned
The clockmaker's time elapsed
The undertaker dug her own grave
Her career? R.I.P
The prison guard has been canned
They slammed the door and set him free

The croupier's been dealt with
Nightclub bouncer shown the door
The chicken farmer got laid off
Clairvoyant's future is unsure
The hairdresser, once permanent
Found out he had been cut
The window of opportunity
For the glazier, has been shut

The cabin crew were shown the exit
The shoe seller got the boot
The butcher went and got the chop
The tailor told he didn't suit
The pilot's turbulent career
Destination has been reached
The midwife's contracted terms
Undelivered, had been breached

The dentist got extracted
Karate master got kicked out
The runner told to walk away
The plumber's job went down the spout
So, it comes as no surprise
It is not so out of whack
Cos every single Christmas Eve
Santa always gets the sack

I am…

I am the greatest
In the world
The world's best
Procrastinator

And, I'll tell you how
It all began…

Nah…
…sod it…
…tell you later!

Ever So Slightly...

...Political

So, during lockdown I started writing a book of poems about the PM and his cabinet in order to point out what, in my humble opinion, was a series of incompetent decisions carried out by increasingly incompetent ministers

I created a world based on a school whereby the PM was the head boy, and other cabinet members were prefects or similar

I gave up writing the book when the behaviour of the cabinet got more and more ridiculous; I quite simply could not keep up!

Some of these poems are included at the beginning of this section

Boris

Boris was a naughty boy
He told lies and broke the rules
He thought he was so clever
And that the other kids were fools
Cos, he didn't need to toe the line
Daddy had seen to that
Cos Daddy knew the principal
And they had had a secret chat

Boris didn't comb his hair
In fact, he made it look a mess
He thought that made him vulnerable
But charming nonetheless
The smarter kids saw through it
Yes, they knew it was a ploy
They thought Boris was ridiculous
Just a silly, scruffy boy

Boris was asked questions
The teacher was incensed
Baffling, babbling, bumbling
Never making any sense
He could not see the reason
For what the teacher would expect
Why should he show maturity?
Why demonstrate respect?

Boris had some hamsters
One for each finger on one hand
Or was it six? No, seven!
Whatever, some of them weren't planned
Of course, he had his favourites
Which he had taken to his heart
The rest were plain ignorable
Cos they did not look the part

Boris, he was lucky
And he got a big surprise
When something crazy happened
Right before his eyes
Cos one day some silly adults
Chose him to be Head Boy
A chance to make a difference
But he chose to destroy

Teacher spoke about a virus
The kids were shocked and sad and scared
But Boris didn't falter
It was like he hadn't heard
He carried on as usual
He laughed and made a joke
Instead of social distancing
He went shaking hands with folk

And Boris got quite poorly
He was soon in some distress
He had to ask for special help
From the special NHS
The doctors and the nurses
They worked all night and day
Until Boris was as right as rain
And then sent him on his way

Well, Boris he was bouncing
His vigour knew no ends
And soon he was back playing
With his closet, richest friends
And they saw an opportunity
Despite the tragedy
To make themselves some pennies
And disregard the misery

So, Boris spread the message
The finest balderdash and pith
He made it complicated
So that the other kids were miffed
And he ensured his buddies
Those bullies with the quids
Could afford to *not* take chances
Leave that to poorer kids

Boris, by his actions
Made it very clear
That the pennies in his pocket
Was all that he held dear
And despite his education
The most expensive in these lands
The silly boy's incompetence
Stained blood upon his hands

The numbers, they kept rising
Ooo, the graphs went up and down
And Boris had to practise
No more smiling, make a frown
Yet still he didn't get it
It was so far beyond his ken
Never lost a wink of sleep
In his bed at number 10

Where Boris loved a party
Or perhaps he maybe did
He wasn't sure what one was
So, he asked another kid
Sue, the perfect prefect,
Asked questions in her perfect way
But somehow found no answers
All areas still were grey

Boris and his buddies
Planned a lucrative attack
Because they knew eventually
Their private tuck shop would be back
They rubbed their hands together
It gave them such a thrill
You see kids – Economies recover
But the dead can't and never will

Boris is a selfish boy
Breaks rules and tells fat lies
Boris is a reckless child
Who does not realise
That the numbers on his death toll
Each one of them; a life
A brother, father, husband
A sister, mother, wife

So, children, when you're older
And you find you have a voice
Think long, think hard, think carefully
Before you make your choice
A baffling, babbling, big buffoon
Might put a smile upon your face
But making one Prime Minister?
Well, that's a national disgrace

Dominic

Dominic was no prefect
But he was always there on hand
Whenever Boris wanted
Something wicked to be planned
Dominic had no reason
Should not have been involved
And yet he made decisions
Which left lots to be resolved

Dominic, he was simple
And treated other kids that way
Used easy-peasy messages
When there was so much more to say
He'd ignore the truth; create a lie
Make things less complicated
Spreading empty promises
These untruths communicated

So, when Boris babbled balderdash
In his incoherent tone
Dominic would strip it down
Right down closely to the bone
Feed Boris silly phrases
Make him repeat them word for word
Between the waffle and the twaddle
Dom's daft messages could be heard

One day a special idea
Made Dominic hellbent
On spreading lying messages
Everywhere that Boris went
Dom dreamt up an awful lie
One he knew would cause a fuss
And in giant letters painted
His twisted words on the school bus

The lie was quite eye-catching
It tugged at people's hearts
As the bus went round and round
Towns and cities, other parts
Sadly, folks believed it
They were sucked in by the lies
So, they let Boris benefit
Only those he'd prioritise

So, Boris got the Head Boy job
Thanks to Dominic's cruel plan
And in return, well, Boris made
Dominic his right-hand man
That meant special privilege
And lashings of leeway
So, Dominic could do anything
And he could do it his own way

But Dominic wanted helpers
To get his harmful mission done
A search for certain people
Was immediately begun
Dominic searched the entire school
For weirdos and for misfits
He set the bar so very low
It truly was the pits

But as he was busy planning
A strange virus came along
He really should have done things right
Yet, got everything so wrong
When his girlfriend got the illness
They sneaked off that very day
Instead of isolating
They went 200 miles away

Yes, Dominic went to Daddy's house
To hell with implication
Clearly saw a chance to take
A crafty school vacation
They should have been in quarantine
Not off and gallivanting
No matter if that cottage was
So cute and so enchanting

The strangest thing, however
Was about a birthday trip
When Dominic was spotted out
He was in line to get some jip
He oddly claimed his sight was bad
And even thought it caused him hassle
The only way to check his eyes
Was to visit Barnard Castle

It was, of course, another lie
One stinking and a-humming
A certain pleasing irony;
Any fool could see it coming
But Dominic knew apologies
Were not needed to attempt
Cos as a special Boris-friend
He was permanently exempt

The kids who wrote the newsletter
Gathered in the school rose garden
So, Dominic could speak to them
Yet, he did not beg their pardon
He fed them with a pack of lies
That story he'd conceived
See Dominic so wrongly thought
That he had been believed

But it didn't really matter
Dominic still kept his job
He was, however, told he should
Learn when to zip his gob
So, quietly he got to work
On the thing he came to do
Redesigning exit routes
Made them red and white and blue

That was his special homework
The only task upon his list
Causing long procedures
That before did not exist
Turns out his simple messaging
Was ridiculous, naïve
And those promises they'd promised?
Got stuffed straight back up his sleeve

So, children here's the lesson
We can all learn from Dominic
Don't speak down to people
Don't lie, don't take the mick
And just don't say it can be done
Cos you'll only prove the rule
Lack of foresight shows you are
A short-sighted, silly fool

Gavin

Gavin thought he had it made
When he got his special role
Student Liaison Officer
It gave him such control
He could make some big decisions
To affect all of the school
All the kids would have to do
What he said was the rule

The power he was given
Well, it went straight up to his head
He could be doing so much good
He planned wicked things instead
He set out to make it tough
For most kids to make top grade
Unless, of course, quite naturally
The highest increments were paid

Things were running smoothly
Gavin kept on devising plans
Until something shocking happened
And he had a problem on his hands
A virus meant the children
The staff and teachers were at risk
Urgent action was then needed
The whole school was in a fix

Gavin hemmed and hawed
He dithered and he dathered
And yet he didn't even look
At the information others gathered
But then, in spontaneity
Along came some inspiration
He could close the whole school down
Wash his hands of obligation

Then some bright spark made a point
There was a flaw in Gavin's plot
How would students leaving school
Get to know the grades they'd got?
Gavin, he was flummoxed
He hadn't thought that far ahead
He preferred academic grades
Were based on privilege instead

"Right, let's make this simple,"
Gavin angrily declared
"No need to fret and worry
No need to get all scared"
We just need some mathematics
A formula, a basic sum
To sort the wheat out from the chaff
The elite from all that scum

"We'll have a well-balanced equation
Done as easily as pie"
He then grabbed pen and paper
Wow, there was no stopping this guy!
"Look, first of all consider
Previous schools kids attended
Multiple by their postcodes
Factor in any rich befriended"

"Take the square root of their social class
Their heritage and pedigrees
Double teacher's estimates
Assuming grandaddy's paid the fees
Plus an extra ten per cent
For each palm-greasing generation
And round it up with evidence
Of blue-blooded line connection"

"Now, those scholarships from lesser homes
That requires a different system
To suggest that we give a dam
But inevitably dismissed 'em
We'll pull the wool over their eyes
Yes, we'll bamboozle them with science
Create a secret algorithm
So confused, they'll give compliance"

"So, take the grades their teachers say
And reduce them by a third
The crazy optimism of their grades
I've seldom seen stuff so absurd!
Next subtract the tax code
Of the highest earner in the house
Deduct five per cent for accents
Brummie, Geordie, Welsh or Scouse"

When the dreaded day arrived
The time for A Level results
The high-class kids all got top marks
The poorer ones just got insults
All that work that they had done
Systematically ignored
Gavin and his formula
Were questioned and deplored

Yes, Gavin had to answer
Questions came so thick and fast
Why were futures jeopardised?
Why ignore the grade forecast?
When teachers gave their estimates
Why'd you not stick with 'em?
Why this unfair attitude?
Well, you can stuff your algorithm

Gavin, sweating uncontrollably
He stumbled on his words
Could not quite admit the truth
His fancy system pumped out turds
He lost so much face and status
And, well, he should have got the sack
But, of course, his job was safe
Cos Head Boy Boris had his back!

There's more to say of Gavin
But for now, we'll leave it there
His approach remains unsuitable
The consequences still unfair
He was asked to maintain standards
Enable each and every kid to learn
But I guess, by his example
Kids know how to stop and then U turn

Wellness Matt

Matt, he was a prefect
Though he wasn't any good
But as a friend of Boris
That didn't matter as it should
So, Matt did next to nothing
Except wear his prefect tie
Which he made the others see
That put a sparkle in his eye

Boris, he had chosen Matt
To be the Student Wellness Rep
That made Matt smirk smugly
And put a spring into his step
"Such a simple, silly duty,"
He was thinking to himself
"Cos no kids truly give a dam
About another pupil's health"

Matt had a special, shiny badge
Upon his blazer it was pinned
He made sure everybody saw it
As he inanely grinned
The clever kids who saw this
Those brighter pupils in the know
Knew the symbolism of Matt's badge
Was plainly just for show

There was so much that Matt could do
To help others feel their best
But Matt, he only cared for friends
He disregarded all the rest
He didn't seem to understand
The positive stuff he could do
In fact, this vacant, vapid, void
Simply did not have a clue

Then, suddenly from nowhere
An important issue came along
An illness harming families
Young and old and weak and strong
This illness was so mighty
It spread right across the school
But Wellness Matt was ready
At least he thought he was, the fool!

Matt could have done some research
So many experts he could ask
The Head of Science waited
To inform Matt about his task
The school nurses were available
To explain and to advise
But Matt gave not a whatsit
So he did not empathise

Cos Wellness Matt – He knew best
He would do it his own way
He stood before the nervous school
What was he going to say?
Well, not a lot as it turned out
He looked serious and concerned
Just to prove he hadn't listened
To all those things he should have learned

There was a need for PPE
Such as visors gloves and masks
To keep matron and the nurses safe
Whilst saving lives with caring tasks
So, Matt got down to business
Private contracts to arrange
For his inexperienced cronies
And he'd let them keep the change

Some bloke Matt knew from down the pub
Was put in charge of PPE
So, a beer mat with elastic bands
The prototype initially
Matron and the nurses
Well, they had to scratch their heads
Wondering what would be done
For their desperate need for beds

Matt said, "Use the corridor
Or make sick kids wait outside"
When told that was incompetent
Well, that was all denied
Matt took no responsibility
He even wanted gratitude
Wondered why the other kids
Despised his attitude

All the kids around the school
They had not a lot to give
To thank the nurses for their actions
Which enabled lucky ones to live
So once a week the school as one
Would stop everything to clap
And think about the efforts made
In all schools across the map

Some clever bloomin' boffins
Found a way to ease the harm
Their super, special safeness
A real shot in the arm
Well Matt, he took the credit
Like all that was his own work
Waited for those top-notch grades
But none forthcoming for this berk

Matt saw an opportunity
When he came across some news
He faked being all emotional
Tried to change the other's views
When asked about protection
Given to that Will Shakespeare
Wellness Matt burst right out crying
Yet he didn't shed a tear

The Head Teacher had some questions
About the way Matt did behave
Especially in relation to
Those private contracts that he gave
See the Head could see no reason
For Matt's complacency
And said Matt should now be punished
There being no transparency

Matt had a chance to make amends
To make up for his mistakes
A chance to make a difference
And to truly up the stakes
Do something for the nurses
Show them what their efforts meant
So Matt, to show appreciation
Gave a great big one per cent

The nurses, rightly, wanted more
All the school kids they agreed
Wondered just how Wellness Matt
Could ignore what they'd achieved
Their selfless, caring actions
Their contributions were so much
How could stupid Wellness Matt
Be so far out of touch?

So children, should you look back
On these tricky virus times
It might not be apparent
What could be read between the lines
History written by our leaders
So often hides the truth
Corruption gets forgotten
As they disregard the proof

Matt the Wellness prefect
Could have stepped up to the mark
Done the gallant thing for once
Shared some light instead of dark
But as before, the privileged bully,
Prioritised little but himself
And compromised the wellness
Of an entire nation's health

Priti

Priti, she was happy
Like the cat that got the cream
When Head Boy Boris told her
She'd got a space within his team
Boris went to Priti
And asked her, "Pretty please
Could you be School House Monitor
In charge of rules and liberties?"

A smile appeared on Priti's lips
A smug, conniving smile
And anyone who saw it knew
It would stay there for a while
Cos Priti's smile hid no secrets
Nor that dark glint in her eyes
It's her way or the highway
No way she's gonna compromise

Priti was a wicked choice
To be put in charge of things
She'd been trusted once before
But been sacked for pulling strings
The former School Head Girl
Had put Priti in a job
Develop Overseas Connections
But she couldn't hold her gob

She had some sneaky meetings
With folk from other schools
Then lied about them happening
Treated everyone like fools
Boris, of course, he knew that
He knew Priti's history
In fact, that's why he like her
No surprise, no mystery

Priti had some strong beliefs
Which she wanted to enforce
She wanted stronger punishments
No questions, no remorse
She believed that those with power
Should have the right to pick and choose
When they didn't like how someone looked
Then they were someone they could lose

Priti knew her ideas
And her selfish policies
Designed to suppress others
Remove opportunities
She formed a ring of prefects
To carry out her dirty work
Whilst she hid herself away
Behind that wicked, callous smirk

Part of Priti's job
Was to welcome each newcomer
Who came from other schools
Throughout winter, spring and summer
But Priti truly hated this
Did not want to see new faces
Preferred to send the newbies back
To the poor and dangerous places

Priti had a vision, see
Of how the school could look
If kids did not fit her view
At them, she'd throw the book
For the smallest indiscretions
She'd enforce imprisonments
And keep people feeling threatened
In her hostile environments

Yes, Priti was a big fan
Of cruel hostility
Did not treat kids with honour
Respect or dignity
See, Priti like a bully
Had a temper, quick to rage
If anyone around her was
Simply on a different page

She got angry at the other kids
Who were sent to give assistance
They could not even speak their minds
Or even think of slight resistance
She'd shout, "I've told you thirty-six
Hundred million twenty-two
Thousand forty-seven times
Exactly what to do!!!"

She'd scream and shout; rant and rave
Be wild, intimidating
Threatening anyone at all
With no sign of contemplating
She'd belittle all the other kids
Call them names and hurl insults
Then wonder why her methods, well
Would not get the best results

At a time when it was very clear
The school needed to enhance
The treatment of some certain kids
And provide an equal chance
She failed to acknowledge
The Black Lives Matters voice
She could have truly helped this cause
But made a callous, selfish choice

You see, Priti was so ignorant
To political unrest
Didn't tolerate it when
Others felt they should protest
But she would get protective
Should a statue come to harm
She thought a statue of a racist
Had a nostalgic kind of charm

Priti was so privileged
That she couldn't see the fact
The way she was behaving
Was a horrid, harmful act
Just because she'd made it
And had no need to ever worry
Didn't mean she could ignore
And dismiss others in a hurry

See, Priti didn't like it
Hated the very thought
That others could have what she had
Preferred others all had nought
And that is why she took away
So many basic, human rights
From all those common, simple kids
That she saw as parasites

Still, there's power in numbers
When the many face the few
Those like Priti panic
And can't think of what to do
When their lies are rightly broken
When common sense can rule the day
There's a social obligation
To stand up and have your say

So, kids please do remember
That if something's not alright
You can still speak up about it
Be bold, be brave, be bright
And should you ever see Ms Priti
You should get your message sent
Be seriously annoying
And seriously inconveni*ent*

Ain't No Party

(Originally a song-cum-sketch, of sorts. Somewhere between and terrible rap and an overly-wordy football chant – vague, voluntary stage directions included!)

There ain't no party
Like a Tory Party
Cos a Tory party goes on (*clap, clap!*)
Yeah, you're the fools
They have no rules
As the Tory party goes on

There ain't no party
Like a Tory Party
Cos a Tory party goes on (*clap, clap!*)
Even in lockdown
Right across the town
A Tory party is second to none

There ain't no party
Like a Tory Party
Cos a Tory party goes on (*clap, clap!*)
Even if restricted
Across the district
But don't go telling anyone

There ain't no party
Like a Tory Party
Cos a Tory party goes on (*clap, clap!*)
Playing party games
Not naming names
Cheese and wine never hurt anyone

There ain't no party
Like a Tory Party
Cos a Tory party goes on (*clap, clap!*)
With a laugh and a joke
And a line of coke
Number of fucks that they give is none

There ain't no party
Like a Tory Party
Cos a Tory party goes on (*clap, clap!*)
They celebrate
Don't isolate
Like the virus has been and gone

There ain't no party
Like a Tory Party
Cos a Tory party goes on (*clap, clap!*)
Booze in place
Within a suitcase
Was it two for the price of one?

(Now, with a dodgy impression of Boris Johnson)

No, Mr Speaker...

There was no party
No Tory party
No Tory party went on
And I've been informed
Rules were not ignored
At the Tory party that never went on

(Now, with a more serious, newsreader tone)

Look,
There is a Party
A Tory Party
And all they do may have you distracted
They've passed legislation
To increase deprivation
It's the vulnerable that are most impacted

There is a Party
A Tory Party
And they partied whilst loved ones died
Their noses are growing
And cracks are showing
Yet, democratic justice is denied

There is a Party
A Tory Party
Your struggles bring them such joy
They don't appear bright
When they're talking shite
But, believe me, all of it's a ploy

There is a Party
A Tory Party
Doing harm every minute, every hour
So, please take note
Don't give them your vote
Socially distance them lot from power

Double

I'm double jab-tastic
Had a shot in the arm
In fact, I've had two
Hope they work like a charm
I'll still wear a mask, though
When I'm out running chores
To protect me and mine
To protect you and yours

My Booster

My booster
Didn't boost me
It kinda
Just reduced me
Made me tired
Made me sleepy
Made me ill
But, if following
The science
Leads to further
Vaccs compliance
Roll me up
Roll up my sleeve
And jab at will

Cos even though
I feel quite shitty
I'll still listen
To Chris Witty
These jabs work
These jabs protect
They're not a farce
But I'll ignore
That crap Prime Minister
Who's so reckless
And so sinister
Talking nonsense
Talking bollocks
Straight out his arse

I'm CoVid Free

I'm CoVid free
I'm CoVid free
Whoop de do
Whoop de de

I'm CoVid free
I'm CoVid free
I'm as happy
As can be

I'm CoVid free
I'm CoVid free
Vaccinations
1, 2, 3

I'm CoVid free
I'm CoVid free
Built up an
Immunity

I'm CoVid free
I'm CoVid free
Pesky virus
Won't get me

I'm CoVid free
I'm CoVid free
Thanks in part
To PPE

I'm CoVid free
I'm CoVid free
I found a test
And there's no fee

I'm CoVid free
I'm CoVid free
I had asparagus
For my tea...

...and my piss stinks!

Checking Out (A Cost of Living Experience)

Adrenaline
A rush of blood
Heart beats faster
Than it should
Fully-loaded
Bags are packed
Do a runner!
Don't turn back!
A price to pay
Is this the time?
Insufficient
In decline?
She looks at me
"Cash or card?"
I make a fist
Clench it hard
Embarrassment
Face goes red
Tap the screen
No words are said
Damn…delay…
Waiting…waiting…
Holding…breath…
Antic…i…pating

Weight on shoulders
Shoppers stare
Desperation
Dark despair
Sweaty palms
Why so slow?
Turn and run
Go, go, go
But, lights go green
Stress; removed
Transaction has
Been approved

Prices Kept on Soaring

She'd always seemed to struggle
Yet somehow made ends meet
Clothed her loving daughter
Put shoes upon her feet
But as prices kept on soaring
Red letters brought the heat
Too much was upon her plate
But none of it to eat
Starved by consequences
Stark choices thick and fast
Her benefits so pitiful
She could barely make them last

They'd always watched their pennies
Always put their children first
Satisfied their hunger
Quenched their every thirst
But as prices kept on soaring
Their pennies weren't enough
Queuing at the foodbank
For proud parents, that was tough
Compromised by consequences
Their marriage showed the strain
The children caught between them
Feeling that they were to blame

She'd always felt triumphant
With the business she had grown
Built it up from nothing
Except the courage she had shown
But as prices kept on soaring
Her overheads were overdue
Closing down her pride and joy
Such a joyless thing to do
Bankrupt by consequences
Depression now; not pride
Not unlike her humble home
She felt empty, cold inside

She'd always been so prudent
Her age made her that way
Rationed by the purse strings
Saved for a rainy day
But as prices kept on soaring
The rainy days became a flood
Her nest egg; broken, shattered
Her good sense did no good
Frozen stiff by consequences
The stress, the strain, the strife
The soaring cost of living
Came to cost her very life

They'd always made a profit
Fat cats fuelled by greed
A bonus in the pipeline
More than they'd ever need
And as prices kept on soaring
They lined their pockets even more
Rubbed their hands together
Energised themselves for sure
Filthy rich by consequences
Their callousness displayed
The soaring cost of living?
That's the windfall they were paid

Originally appeared in...Nobody Left Behind (2023)
(Printed Words, Edited by Amanda Nicholson)
An Anthology in aid of Mustard Tree
and in response to the cost of living crisis

Cutbacks

I've had to cutback
Now money's so tight
The cost of living
Has come home to bite
I wake in the morning
The first thought in my head
How much could I save
If I just stayed in bed?
I'm quicker than ever
When taking a shower
I need to be clean
But I need to save power
My clever smart speaker
Unplugged at the wall
Doesn't take orders
Or instructions at all
I limit the telly
Only watching the news
But then get annoyed
By political views
I'm wearing thick jumpers
Two socks on each foot
Still quiver, still shiver
Still freezing my butt

I've got radiators
They're pure decoration
The only thing bleeding?
My bloody vexation!
If I ignite the gas fire
I see burning pound notes
So, I've fashioned a blanket
Out of old overcoats
I used to eat steak
With an egg that I'd fry
Knocked that on the head
Cos the stakes are so high
My meat and two veg
Has become meat and one
I can't afford butter
To butter my scone
At the supermarket
I dash with my trolley
Straight past the cakes
And other such folly
I don't leave the house
For a social occasion
It's not about tax
It's expenses evasion!

We've all made cutbacks
All made sacrifices
Not buying as much
Not using devices
Just first world problems?
Still, problems are felt
As we tighten our grip
As we tighten our belt
But short-lived hardship
Perhaps trivial pain
Be mindful; think on
It's so much worse in Ukraine

Watching Question Time

Oh, get on with it, man
Enough of this natter
Nevermind, "And now the weather
With Tomasz Schafernaker
Get the politics on
I've got anger to vent
And woe be tide anyone
Of a right wing bent

Ah, there it is
That familiar tune
It'll be "Hello and welcome,"
From Fiona Bruce soon
"This week we're live
On Question Time"
From, like, Bognor Regis,
Or Newcastle upon Tyne

Introducing the panel
Each one in turn
Some halfway decent
But most fit to burn
There's an inbred Tory
With no chin and no ethics
From a backward backwater
Somewhere in Essex

Oh look, a Lib Dem!
Of all things to appear
Must have an eye on
A presenting career
Some random director
From a massive chain store
Pretending to care about
The needy and poor

And with this Labour MP
They could be an adventure
Cos she can never decide
If she's left, right or centre
And perched on the end
To show impartiality
There's a right-wing nutter
Typical BBC

OK, question one
Comes in from the crowd
Wait for the microphone
So you're heard clear and loud
Good question for starters
I have to confess
Raising an issue
The panel needs to address

The Lib Dem goes first
But doesn't say much
Uninspiring and dull
And plain out of touch
Look! It's an obvious question
Do your research
Lazy MPs like you
Drive me berserk

Then the business leader
With his tuppence worth
His sweatshop's top rate
For an entire week's work
He then proves beyond doubt
That he only cares for himself
In favour of all the cuts
To the National Health

Whoa! The right-wing nutter
Is already fuming
About to blame immigrants
I'm already assuming
"There are too many foreigners
We're full to the top"
Oi! Without immigration
This country's at a full stop

Next, Lord Chinless the Tory
With a change of direction
But only because
He's avoiding the question
Show some respect man!
You ignorant arse
Complete muppets like you
Make this whole thing a farce

The Labour MP?
Well, she gets the last word
And after all of this time
Should have something prepared
"It's not my party's fault
Cos we're not in power"
Well, that was a bit pointless
Not you're finest hour

The questions keep coming
But they're dodged and ignored
The day's biggest issues
Are left unexplored
There's no accountability
No one's taken to task
It's seemingly irrelevant
That the questions are asked

Is this claptrap the best
The BBC can contrive?
It's the same every week
Approx 10:45
And yet somehow it remains
A firm favourite of mine
That infuriating experience
Watching Question Time

Ever So Slightly...
...Thoughtful

The poems Families, Religions, Be Kind, *and* In Common *originally appeared in* Lucy the Tooth Fairy's Last Chance (2020)

This is collection of my illustrated poems aimed at children but which are also be enjoyed by those who are young at heart

Sometimes

Sometimes you gotta roll the dice
Sometimes you gotta chance your arm
Sometimes you gotta trust yourself
And not your lucky charm

Sometimes you have to have a go
Sometimes you have to hope and see
Sometimes you have to take the plunge
To change your destiny

Sometimes you need to risk it
Sometimes you need to try
Sometimes you need to look beyond
What firstly meets your eye

Sometimes if you wait too long
Sometimes if you hesitate
Sometime if you play it safe
You can over-contemplate

So, each time that you doubt yourself
Each time you're not so sure
Each time there's an option, ask
"Could I be better than before?"

Families

Have you got two mamas?
Have you got two papas?
Do you happen to have one of each?
Do you have a home with mother?
Does you dad have another?
But you get to go and see him every week?

Or is it, dependable Dad
Who's back at your pad?
Making sure that you sleep and you eat?
Is it Auntie or Grandma?
Your uncle, your grandpa?
Who's helping you find your own feet?

Are you currently fostered?
Have you been adopted?
Got a new loving family of your own?
Got brothers and sisters
From other mothers and misters?
Or an only child who's happy alone?

Do you...
...need to be stronger?
Cos your mummy's no longer?
Does your daddy look on from above?
Well, all families are different
With one thing consistent
They're all held together with love

Can You...?

Can you have a hug without another?
Can you shake hands with empty space?
Can you blow a kiss from miles away
To land on a loved one's face?

Can you spare a thought for someone?
Can you keep someone in mind?
Cos if you can you'll put the kindness
Back into humankind

..ness

If you bumble round with bumbleness
Then tumble down with tumbleness
But humbly have humbleness
Not grumble, gripe with grumbleness
Perhaps no one clocks your clumsiness

Religions

Have you got special ways?
And festival days
Which are different to others you know?
Are there foods you can't eat
Such as certain meat
Cos it's a sacred, religious no-go?

Wear different clothes
From your head to your toes?
For reasons that matter to you?
Are others aware
When you say a prayer
It's just one of those things that you do?

Do you sometimes confuse
Which language to use
Depending on each conversation?
Or, in your point of view
Faith's not for you
But you understand and you show toleration?

So, at Diwali, at Eid
Yom Kippur, yes indeed
At Baisakhi and on the Day of the Buddha
And on Christmas Day
It's important to say
We should love and respect one another

Halfway Up

Don't be pessimistic
If you've had a lousy day
If from morning until midnight
Nothing's gone your way
If everything you tried to do
Seemed to turn out bad
When looking back and pondering
You simply curse the luck you had

Try to look in detail
Try to see things differently
There could be something hidden
Like a tiny victory
Sometimes you may think you lose
But in many ways, you win
Cos failing isn't ending, see
It's a new chance to begin

So, at times when you look at life
As if your glass is far from full
Reach on down and grab your socks
Give them a mighty pull
Each day brings new challenges
But we shouldn't let them thwart us
So, today's glass was but halfway up
Could tomorrow's be three quarters?

Be Kind

From time to time
Do you see online
That people have said something cruel?
What would you do
If said about you?
Get angry and feel like a fool?

Are you concerned
Now that you've learned
That others can choose to be mean?
Bullies don't care
If a selfie you share
Is turned to a horrible meme

Have you instead
Joined in on a thread
Where banter has gone way too far?
Laughing out loud?
Just part of the crowd
Despite knowing that comments can scar?

You do have a choice
When using your voice
So, it's time to make up your mind
Please make a note
Remember this quote
In a world where you can be anything; be kind

I Once Stood

I once stood in a space
That wasn't a place
Not in the true, real sense
Nowhere but somewhere
Stillness and stale air
Accessed through a hole in a fence

Both left, right a tower
Those symbols of power
Built from a threatening stone
Where soldiers on guard
Without a regard
Shot freely at persons unknown

Not East, yet, not West
A place to contest?
A land was divided; a wall
Simple line on a chart
Tore families apart
Til the day the oppression did fall

Just two years before
Because of an old war
Where I stood was a land for no man
Now plain, open field
With history concealed
That twisted and damaging plan

If I'd stood on that turf
That cold lump of earth
I would have been under attack
Due to repression
A trigger's depression
Be shot in the front, same as back

And as I stood there
With a change in the air
One foot in the now, one the past
Two nations combined
Their future's aligned
Unity forged, built to last

As it happened, that day
I turned, walked away
Whereas many, shot dead, never could
The boundary removed
Liberty then improved
Yet history stands in that place I once stood

In Common

What do you do
You see someone new?
Sometimes it's hard to begin
First thing you see
May happen to be
The colour of that person's skin

Look at their eyes
You may realise
That they're the same colour as yours
Their mouth, ears and nose
The way their hair grows
All quite familiar, of course

A dimply chin?
A nice, cheeky grin?
A smile with a missing front tooth?
Kind-hearted face
With trust and with grace
And lips that will tell you the truth?

Different, that's right!
Ah yes, but not quite
Don't judge with your eyes use your heart
And no need to fuss
Cos you, me and us
Have more in common than sets us apart

Some Walls

Some walls are high and mighty
Some walls are small but strong
Some walls are short in distance
Some walls reach all along
Some walls are temporary
Some walls are built to last
Some walls are for the future
Some walls are from the past
Some walls are built as borders
Some walls mark out a place
Some walls are for protection
One can be seen from outer space

Some walls are only make believe
These walls are shame and fear and pride
These walls we build up on our own
These walls keep us trapped inside
These walls can make us nervous
These walls make us shy, annoyed
These walls can be broken down
These walls can be smashed, destroyed
These walls, they form no barrier
These walls crumble to the ground
These walls are insignificant
When our inner strength is found

Simply, R.I.P

I'm an atheist
Who celebrates at Christmas
A non-believer
Who respects every faith and creed
An anti-fascist
Who wants equality and fairness
Anti-capitalist
With sporadic signs of greed

Not homophobic
I believe people should love freely
Anti-racist
I find intolerance obscene
Anti-hatred
I have much love for people
Anti-royalist
Yet, I'll kind of miss the Queen

Against words
Like majesty or highness
You will not hear
An H.R.H from me
But you were loved
Admired and respected
So, Elizabeth
May you simply R.I.P

Ever So Slightly...

...Smutty

Slaughterhouse Love

When he first saw her
Kyle was lamb to the slaughter
Felt the pumping of blood
And the stirring of water
He'd watch her fine skills
In that abattoir
Her slashing; her chopping
Her whole repertoire

He'd be weak at the knees
Be all of a quiver
Watching her slicing
Intestines and liver
As she hung up a carcass
He was hung up on Kate
His lust had no end
There was no sell by date

She was confident too
She did not mince her words
Even covered in offal
And the gizzards of birds
Her grace and her beauty
Had Kyle so besotted
Especially when he saw
That pig get garrotted

He plucked up the courage
His nerves all a jangle
Meat sweats in his palms
His guts in a tangle
He asked whether Kate
Would, just for one night
Risk it for a brisket
And hook up for a bite

Kyle supersized it
Just proving his point
Went to town, the best end
Not some cheap greasy joint
They had a banger of a night
And no bones about that
With some harmless ribbing
Whilst chewing the fat

A few dates went by
And the heat it got higher
The couple, in fact
Were soon cooking on fire
Kate said, "I've fallen
Fallen for you really deep
I give you my heart
And the lungs from that sheep"

But soon Kyle was distracted
To his own surprise
Temptation of flesh with
Tender breasts, legs and thighs
A new girl named Maureen
Piqued his int'rest
Covered in giblets
In blooded clothes she was dressed

Kyle starting flirting
He weighed in by the scales
Provocative motions
With a pile of entrails
He gave Maureen sweetbreads
To sweeten her mood
If Kate had a butcher's
He'd get barbecued

Kyle, went too far
He knew not when to stop
Kate soon had beef
He was up for the chop
She'd have his guts for garters
She'd skin him alive
It was what she did best
Each day; nine to five

Aye, he'd gotten her goat
He'd given her gripe
She was up in his grill
Had enough of this tripe
She sharpened her knives
A plan was a-stewing
Giving Maureen the eyes
Would be Kyle's undoing

Kate crept up on Kyle
Smooth, accurate, quick
With a flick of the wrist
She whipped off his dick
The reason for this?
Well, to act as a caution
Cos no one but Kate
Was to sample Kyle's portion

My and Your

My nether regions
Your private parts
My special area
Your Bakewell tarts

Your kept-under-wraps
My trouser dwellers
Your you-know-what
My unemployed fellas

My jingle-jangles
Your secret down under
My wobbly bits
Your I'm-left-to-wonder

Your mind-your-own-business
My under-the-covers
Your Maid of Your Honour
My friend and his brothers

Your hu-ha, your whatsit
A sight for sore eyes
My do-da, my 'That's it!"
With audible sighs

Your crikey, your blimey
A sight to behold
My sorry, my whoopsy
Cos, baby it's cold

Let's get them together
Let's try it one night
Yeah, you're out of my league
It's too bad, but alright!

Smutty Limericks I

He simply could not compete
That thing had him totally beat
Every setting and speed
Would always succeed
That device that his wife kept discreet

You may well feel like a clown
Or damage your best nightgown
Cos if you feel frisky
It can be so risky
If the Kama Sutra is held upside down

Now, he was on a promise, she said
So, handcuffed himself to the bed
But then through the door
His Mother-in-Law
Came into the bedroom instead

Her fantasy, she had fessed up
Was to see her hubby dressed up
But what he did; she din't like
Cos he thought Magic Mike
Was a magician – he'd truly messed up

Harry and Joan

"There's nowt on the telly,"
Says Harry to Joan
"Everything they're showing
They've already shown
So, I've searched high and low
Through the channels from Sky
And there are quite a few films
That have quite caught my eye"

"There's Missionary Impossible
A spy film with a twist
Not sure what's been twisted
But I think I get the gist
White Men Can't Hump
A shy basketball player
There's a film about Buffy
Who's a Vampire Layer"

"There's The Extra Testicle?
A new take on ET
And The Slutty Professor?
She's a PhD!
The Tale of Throbbin' Hood?
Could be well worth a look
Though not so why they've changed his mate's name to …
…Triar F F F forget that one!"

"There's Legally Boned?
And American Booty?
The Porn Identity?
But that sounds a bit fruity
A Tale of Two…. Titties?
Oh my, what the Dickens
See plenty of choice, love
It's hardly slim pickings

"Sperminator? Drill Bill?
Forest Hump? Boobarella?
Top Buns? Twin Cheeks?
Original Sin …da-rella
Loads you can choose from
No need to be fussy
The only thing on Freeview's
Is that Bond – Octopussy"

"OK, Trannie Get Your Gun?
It must discuss gender issues
And must be emotional
They recommend using tissues
There's Jurassic Pork?
C'mon, you love dinosaurs
How about Frisky Business?
Game of Bones? Bra Wars?"

"My Bare Lady – Classic
Oh, it's in black and white
There's another oldie
Tits a Wonderful Life!
There's Shaving Ryan's Privates?
But I think that's just an interpretation
Of a surgical procedure
Before a major operation"

"There's Wild, Wild Chest?
Pulp Friction and more
Like – Inspect Her Gadget
(Wowzers – seen that one before)
Saturday Night Beaver?
Good Will Humping too?
Look, whatever you fancy
I'll leave it you"

"Come here," says Joan
As she grabs the remote
"You know none of these films
Will quite float my boat
Cos I only love watching
As phallus by phallus
My favourite star Debbie
Well and truly Does Dallas"

How About it?

Rumpy-pumpy
Bounce me, bump me
Let's take this upstairs
Hanky-panky
Slap me, spank me
The daring-est of dares

Big time lovers
Between the covers
Let's roll in the hay
Pringle, prickle
Slap and tickle
Wickedest wicked way

Whips and chains
Sexy games
Tricks to stimulate
Be complicit
Be explicit
Toys set to vibrate

My sex buddy
In the nuddy
Orgasmic satisfaction
Not meek, not mild
Let's go wild
Driven by attraction

Let's get rude
You in the mood?
How about it? Me and you?
What, not tonight?
Well, that's alright
Yeah, I've got a headache too!

Smutty Limericks II

I don't care if you beg and you pray
We're not gonna do it that way
Quit your complaining
I'm done with explaining
Case closed - There's no more to say

Shaking and weak at the knees
Dancing a sexy striptease
But the mood got shattered
And bedsheets got splattered
With a massive, mucus-filled sneeze

At first, he was feeling so bold
His sex drive could not be controlled
But it being so chilly
It effected his willy
Which gave up the ghost in the cold

He said he had purest intention
When attending the nudist convention
But his cover was blown
When bare bodies were shown
A small part of him stood to attention

Bobby and The Lovebot 3000

"Hello, can I help you?"
Said the girl on the line
Bobby sighed with relief
Said "It's about bloody time,
"Twenty-five minutes
I've been held in a queue
And with that so-called music
Look, I've things to do"

"I've called to complain
About this damned contraption
Which was an impulse buy
An instant attraction
But the truth of the matter
Which has left me non-plussed
Is the blasted thing's broken
It's not working. It's bust"

"I'm sorry to hear that,"
The girl sympathised
Bobby was doubtful
He just rolled his eyes
"Do tell me the product
To which you refer
More details are better
The make, model and year"

"It's the Lovebot 3000
And it's the latest one too
With all added extras
But it just will not do
I've unpacked her, unwrapped her
I gave her a name
I've dressed her up pretty
But she won't play the game"

"Ah, the Lovebot 3000
Sir, a wonderful choice
So curvy, so sexy
And with that soft, husky voice
She's state of the art
She'll attend to your needs
With all that good loving
And some down, dirty deeds"

"Well, so far there's nothing,"
Bobby explained,
"There's supposed to be action."
He further complained
"I wanted the Lovebot
With come to bed eyes
And the promise of ecstasy
As advertised"

"I wanted unbridled passion
Hot sex on demand
I've cancelled appointments
I had other things planned
I was sold on positions
On the turn of a dial
But there's no reverse-cowgirl
And there's no doggy-style"

"I'm stuck with this lump
This oversized toy
I'm so disappointed
I expected such joy
Well, I want a refund
All my money back
I've got consumer rights
As a matter of fact"

The girl asked a question
To continue the call
"You're aware she'll need charging?
Have you tried that at all?
You'll find a plug with a lead,
A power pack with a light
Hook her up for one hour
And she'll be at it all night"

"Do you have further questions?"
The girl then enquired
But the line had gone dead
So, she guessed none were required
Bobby had hung up
And dashed off instead
Grabbed the Lovebot 3000
And plug her in by his bed

Smutty Limericks III

There once was a lady called Mary
Who found hair removal so scary
She tried at the spa
But the pain went too far
And now she's been left halfway hairy

There once was a husband called Bill
Who could always please his wife, Jill
Got it up every time
Cos he'd found online
That magical, potent blue pill

He approached her to take up his chance
And asked if she'd like to dance
She told him, "Get stuffed!"
Cos she'd had enough
Of blokes trying to get in her pants

His clothes were all over the lawn
Most of them ripped up and torn
He'd forgotten, you see
To delete his-tor-y
The last time he'd been looking at porn

A to Z (and Back Again)

More a failed experiment than a poem. This was meant to be clever ditty written by using one word at a time in alphabetical order. Of course, that's really difficult to do, well, I found it tricky anyway. So, I cheated....a lot!

Albert	randy,	quickly
becomes	she	passion
cantankerous	tempts	opportunity
dead	until	Nooky!
easily.	voluptuously	Mischief!
Fred	wantingly	Lovemaking!
goads	X-ratedly	Kinkiness!
him	yonder	Justifiably
inciting	zipper	in
jealously.	yawns	her
Kathleen	'xpecting	gift.
loves	waiting	Fred
men	vivaciously	extremely
needling	Unabashed.	drunk
over	The	cannot
passion.	suiters	brandish
Quite	realise	'ard-on!

Ever So Slightly...

...Lovey-Dovey

If It...

If it tickles your fancy
If it floats your boat
If it ticks your boxes
If it gets your vote

If, down to the ground,
It's right up your street
If, all things considered,
It makes you complete

If it starts your motor
If it flutters your heart
If it races your pulse
If it goes off the chart

If it drives you crazy
If it sends you mad
If it colours you happy
Then, it can't be so bad

Cos, if it gets you going
If you try but can't stop
If it wears you out
Til you're fit to drop

If it's reason to live
If it stops you stone dead
If, out of the blue,
You could paint the town red

If you're head over heals
With you heart on your sleeve
If you're gobsmacked, dumbfounded
If it's hard to believe

If it raises you up
If, good heavens above
It does all this to you
Then surely, it's love

Loving Ways

I do not care for kidneys
Give little thought to spleen
An appendix just wobbles round
And is seldom ever seen
Ligaments hold no attachment
Sinews aren't so great
Essential fatty acids
Simply don't hold any weight
I've no interest in arteries
Nor intestines large or small
Blood cells white or red
Don't get me flowing, not at all
But, to put it anatomical,
Here is my point of view
I wonder why it is I love
I love the bones of you

I do not care for fragments
Give not a jot for jots
A snippet's just a tiny part
Of bigger specks and spots
Slivers, shards and smithereens
Simply something incomplete
Chips and chunks and chuck-aways
For me cannot compete
Many minute morsels
Smaller scraps of bigger stuff
Hardly do much for me
Never ever been enough
To take it all apart then
To see just how it fits
I wonder why I love
I love yourself to bits

I do not care for planets
Give no regard to stars
Venus, when upon my chart
Is much the same as Mars
Black holes, quasars, comets
Asteroids placed in a belt
Maybe astronomical
But my heart could hardly melt
Intergalactic missions
Right across the universe?
Beam me down to terra firma
I could think of nothing worse
But for bringing me back down to Earth
For putting me on track
There's no wonder why I love
I love you to the moon and back

Almost, Not Quite

Almost, not quite workaholic
Cos that would be a full-time job
Almost, not quite chocoholic
Get a boost from a hobnob
Almost, not quite alcoholic
The bubbles burst, went flat
Almost not quite shopaholic
Max'd the credit cards with that
Almost, not quite TV addict
Cos I channelled my control
Almost not quite heavy smoker
Cos I lost the need to roll
Almost, not quite fashion victim
Cos the styles began to clash
Almost, not quite adrenalized
Cos I crave the chance to crash
Almost, not quite attention-mad
Now, I'm happily ignored
Almost, not quite dancing craze
Cos that hardly strikes a chord
Almost, not quite a bookie's dream
Cos that slipped away my wealth
Almost, not quite obsessed with you
Now, I've learned to love myself

Said One to Another...

There's not much room
In my mushroom
But you can call to visit
I'll make some room
In my mushroom
Cos that's no trouble, is it?
Cos my mushroom
Is your mushroom
Where you can feel at home
I'll find the room
In my mushroom
Cos you're my favourite gnome

...And Then Said the Other

Is there room
In your mushroom?
Forgive me being nosy
With not much room
In your mushroom
Well, that could be quite cosy
Please make room
In your mushroom
Then we can be together
We'll share the room
In our mushroom
Be home sweet gnome forever

Progress

The world's on my shoulders, it should be at my feet
I try and smile, try to be gracious in defeat
But as it turns out, it's funny in a way
I'll only see tomorrow if I make it through today

I've got a key in the palm of my hand
It opens up nothing, that's all I understand
If I could find a door and have someone let me in
Maybe I'll discover where it is I should begin

Yesterday I was sorry, today I'm pitiful
Tomorrow I'll be happy, in the future be grateful
When we were together, forever side my side
Now you're gone I've got nothing, nothing not even pride

But, now...

I've straightened my shoulders
Standing tall on my feet
These days I'm smiling
I even laugh at your deceit
And, as it turned out
It was funny in a way
I made it to tomorrow
So, goodbye to yesterday

Originally appeared in Dreams of the Night, United Press, 2007

Focus

I took a picture
Of you and me
But it came out
Differently
Tried to remember
What I just saw
I felt as though
I'd been before
I asked you
If you could explain
Said your perception
Was just the same

I saw a movie
I watched the screen
Don't understand
What I have seen
I read the screenplay
Checked out the book
Don't understand
What I mistook
Was it because
You were there?
These days I
Take you everywhere

There's added colour
Between the light
Life's no longer
So black, so white
But if I've
Got sunshine
Will it still rain?
Or will the brightness
Increase my pain?

Originally appeared in, National Poetry Anthology, United Press, 2008

When the Snooker's On

I think of you when the snooker's om
You were potty about the game
It would get your full attention
With yours-truly out the frame
Right on cue, at break off time
Boys on the baize all set to go
Silence was demanded
Without cushioning the blow
You'd react to long pots, short pots
Shots called foul, shots called a miss
I was hampered, I was snookered
No chance of single, double kiss

I think of you when the snooker's on
From all angles, makes me think
Are you feeling blue or green with envy
Are you browned off or tickled pink
Are you in the red or in the black?
Is your life all yellow mellow
Did all the balls fall into place?
Do you rest with a matched bedfellow?
Did you have a romance like a whirlwind
Like a hurricane, like a rocket?
Or kept it simple, played it safe
Your heart left by your pocket?

I think of you when the snooker's on
In fact, I do so now and then
We could turn the table, turn back time
Try not to screw it up again
Have a re-rack, chalk it up
Stun ourselves back on the spot
Play for perfect placement
Line it up and have a shot
So come on and build some bridges
An opportunity left to take
I think of you when the snooker's on
It's been a while – let's end the break

To Be

To be loved
Be beloved
To be loved
To be free

Be assured
Be as sure
As assurance
Can be

And
Realise
Real eyes
Realise
Real lies

Then
Be loved
Be beloved
Be loved
Be set free

But to fly
Butterfly
Yes, to fly
Butterfly
To be free

Ever So Slightly...

...Random

The poems Happy *and* Questions
originally appeared in
The Silly Sausage Saga (2018)

The poems Sad *and* Ambition *originally appeared in*
Lucy the Tooth Fairy's Last Chance (2020)

These are collections of my illustrated poems aimed at children but which
are also enjoyed by those who are young at heart

Well...

I mustn't grumble
Can't complain
I'm not too bad
I'm much the same

I'm fair to middle
I'm well enough
None-to-shabby
New day, same stuff

I'm ticking over
I'm plodding on
Another day
Has been and gone

So, all in all
I guess I'll do
Thanks for asking
And, how are you?

Happy

I'm over the moon
I'm tinkled pink
Buzzin' with life in fact
I'm happy as Larry
Pleased as punch
Grinning like a Cheshire cat

I'm walking on air
I'm chuffed to bits
I'm full of the joys of spring
On top of the world
I'm cock-a-hoop
My heart just wants to sing

Head over heels
I'm up sky high
Footloose and fancy free
I'll say it once more
In case you don't know
I'm as happy as I can be

Sad

I'm down, I'm glum
Unhappy, so bad
I'm blue
I'm low
I'm depressed, so sad

Down in the mouth
Down in the dumps
All out of sorts
I'm such a grumps

Sulky, stroppy
Down hearted, not right
Moody
Gloomy
All darkness, no light

Eh?

I'm baffled
Bamboozled
Befuddled
Bemused
Mixed up
Messed up
Shaken
Confused

Head spinning
Mind swimming
Been knocked for a six
Thoughts fuzzy
Brain buzzy
Caught up in a fix

Too much information
Can't take it all in
Deep breath, clear mind
On my marks
...set
...begin

~~Autocarrot~~ Autocorrect

Hay autocorrect!
Weave bin hear bee four
You chews the wrong options
I'm Sir Ten, I'm shore
Your acting on porpoise
Too make me luck silly
Ran Dom Lee changing
Words Will and illy
I under stand Grandma
I no how two spel
Is it to much too ask
That you wood as well?
Sew pullup you're socks
Sought you're shelf out
Oar yore get ting flung
Write down the sprout

Blah

I'm kinda blah
I'm kinda dah
I'm kinda you know what

I'm outta erm
I'm outta um
I'm outta what I've not

I'm neither neh
Nor neither meh
I'm neither here nor there

I've got no tssh
I've got no sssh
I've go no wing, no prayer

I'm a wee bit ooh
I'm a wee bit aah
I'm a wee bit, 'don't ask me'

I'm lost for oomph
I'm lost for pfft
Cos, I'm lost for words, you see

Questions

Can aliens speak in English?
Is the moon made out of cheese?
Does the sun go up and down?
Does Batman ever sneeze?
Will tomorrow ever get here?
Are all humans in a race?
Where do rainbows go to hide?
And does it rain in space?

Does money ever grow on trees?
Are all trees made from wood?
Can fish swim backwards in reverse?
Would they try it if they could?
Do dogs know what their names are?
Do some choose them for themselves?
Is there such a thing as magic?
Are there fairies, gnomes and elves?

Do farmers wear pyjamas?
Can pigeons watch TV?
Can squares turn into circles?
Am I the only one of me?
Do winners know they're winning?
Do losers know they're last?
And if questions go unanswered
Then I'm so sorry that I asked

Ambition

I'll live forever, if I can
As a vampire or a bogeyman
Or I'll come back as a scary ghost
And haunt my favourite telly host
I could get my face in the hall of fame
Score a goal in a World Cup game
I could go down in history
As an unsolved mystery

I could make a name for myself
Amass fortune, an endless wealth
Be courageous, strong and proud
I'd stand out within a crowd
I could be big, be headline news
Have fancy clothes, designer shoes
A car the size of a massive bus
Adoring fans who'd make a fuss

I could fly off to outer space
Leave behind this earthly place
Be a famous astronaut
Or a hotshot lawyer inside crown court
I could be the one on TV
Who spells out our liberty
Elected chief of the UN
Reincarnate and live again

If I for once just used my mind
Achieved some good for all mankind
Just sat up and had a go
Tried to reap what others sow
Stand up, speak out and stir debate
So they'll never underestimate
The one they thought they could ignore
That extra-ordinary, kid next door

Poems

I write poems
I write them all the time
And when I write poems
I always make them rhyme
Cos, if the sounds don't match
In poems of mine
I worry that they might but somewhat anti-climatic

Here We Go

Well, here we go
Been put on again
Only get worn
Every now, every then

There must be a reason
There must be a match
It's the only occasion
When I leave my patch

I never get washed
Don't even get rinsed
I've got magical powers
At least *he's* convinced

I'm baggy, I'm grubby
I'm unpicked at the seam
But off we both go
Supporting the team

All the jumping and bouncing
In the hot, sweaty crowd
Just adds to my problems
For crying out loud

The stress takes its toll
Each minute, both halves
I get no fresh air
Unlike those waving scarves

The team, they play dreadful
No style, grace or gloss
At the end of the match
It's put down as a loss

He's angry, he's moaning
Recalling the game
The worst thing about it?
He thinks *I'm* to blame

"It's your fault, you loser!"
He raves and he rants
I say, "Grow up,
There's no such thing as lucky pants!"

Swanning Off

I'm swanning off to Swansea
Gonna head to Headingly
I'm skipping down to Skipton
Cantering to Canterb'ry
I'm running off to Runnymede
Gonna rush to Rushden Town
I'm bolting on to Bolton
Counting down to County Down

I'm ambling to Ambleside
Gonna go, go, go Glasgow
I'm pressing on to Preston
Paddling to Port Padstow
I'm burning off to Burnley
Pattering to Patterdale
I'm waltzing off to Walsall
Sailing slowly south to Sale

I'm winging it to Wingham
Off to Wrexham, recklessly
Brum, brum, brum to Birmingham
Angling for Anglesey
Tipping down to Tipperary
Regretting Gretna Green
Doubling back to Dublin
About turn in Aberdeen

Heading hastily to Hastings
Careering down to Cardiff Bay
I'm dipping in and out of Bath
Harping on to Harpurhey
I'm bogging off to Bognor
Getting done down in Dundee
Or perhaps I'll use a Satnav
To better get from A to B

Look Ahead

Look up for inspiration
Look down in preparation
Look high, look wide
Look side to side
Look out with trepidation

Head up for elevation
Head down, determination
Head now, head then
Head back again
Head to your destination

Ray Douglas is primarily a children's author, poet and illustrator who can often be found entertaining kids at schools, libraries and other community locations

 Mr Ray Douglas

 @mrraydouglas1

 @mrraydouglas

 Ray Douglas Kids Poet

 @mrraydouglas

www.raydouglaspoet.co.uk

Children's Books Available on Amazon

The Silly Sausage Saga
and Other Silly Rhymes

hopes to put a smile on a face, a thought in a mind and a laugh in the air. The story of Silly Sausage trying to escape being eaten is told throughout the book along with, as the title suggests, lots of other silly rhymes!

Lucy The Tooth Fairy's Last Chance
and Some Pretty, Witty Ditties

is an illustrated children's book containing oodles of rhymes and poems about all kinds of things. Great for all ages with more than enough to get kids thinking, smiling, laughing and, ultimately interested in and entertained by rhymes and poems

Gold Medal Hunters
Furry Firsts, Feathery Fails

Can Henrietta Hippo ice dance like champ?
Can Oswald the Ostrich jump all the way to glory?
Can Kangaroo Rita hurdle to gold?
Can a team of penguins break bobsleigh barriers?

There's an Egg in the Garden

A young boy looks in the back garden and sees a mysterious egg.
He wonders what can be inside
Will it be a monster? An animal? A bird? A dragon?
A children's picture book story about the nerves and excitement we all feel when trying to make friends

Goodbye

I'll be off then
Cheerio
See you later
Gotta go
Tar-ra for now
Back anon
By which I mean
Later on

Be lucky, stay safe
Bye bye, ta-ta
Don't you go changing
Stay as you are
Toodle-pip people
So long, adieu
Until the next time
Take care of you